AF255915

A Soldier's Soldier

Neysa Holmes, PhD

To my mother. You will always be my light.

To my husband, Erick. I love you more than you will ever know. There will NEVER be ANOTHER... 1 Corinthians 13 - Love is patient... Love is Kind.

To my children and grandchildren, I love you, and I am sorry for my absence over the past few years. I not only had to heal from my own trauma but needed to understand how our system has failed so many and took so many lives. I found that my purpose was beyond my own understanding. This book would not be possible without my journey of healing. Through this process, I was able to forgive and learned to truly love without judgment.

Remember to always ask God to heal your heart, as He is the one who designed it. Ask Him to mend it, and to help you to forgive the person(s) who hurt you. By doing so, you will always find peace.

To all the families that have lost loved ones resulting from war. Not only those who lost service members due to combat casualties, but also to those who lost their loved one on the home front because of addiction and suicide. I am sorry that the government they served so selflessly failed them.

To the wives and families of Special Operators.

To Ilchi Lee and his philosophy of healing. Your profound work helped me to understanding my self-worth and my purpose in life. I will always be grateful to you for teaching me the importance of healing my brain and body. Through this process, I have been able to share with others your books and help others address their own deep-embedded trauma.

To Lakshmi Delbel, no words – just gratitude.

To Dr. Christopher Frueh for your commitment to addressing "Operator Syndrome."

To my family and friends who never questioned my commitment and love for Erick.

Acknowledgments

First, I must thank God for his mercy, grace, and never wavering love. We are to walk by faith and not by sight. We must keep our faith when we praise God in the storm. We are to trust him in the valley and follow him in the dark.

I want to thank Erick for this journey. This book would not be possible without you. The service and sacrifices that you and others gave for this country will forever be honored.

To the late Toby Keith, for his support of our troops and our veterans. So many do not understand the sacrifices of the "American Soldier," and you honored them throughout your career. Thank you, Sir.

Dolly Parton, Thank you for your rendition of The Ballet of the Green Beret.

A special thanks to other country music artists who have allowed us to continue to love one another even during our darkest times. Through your songs, we kept our deep faith in God alive and were able to hold on to a bond that was formed as children.

Thank you to the following artists and their music that kept THIS fire burning:

FGL for Dirt; Josh Turner for Hometown Girl; Scotty McCreery for 5 More Minutes and This is It; Morgan Wallen for This Side of a Dust Cloud, Wine Into Water, Only Thing That's Gone with Chris Stapleton, Man Made a Bar with Eric Church; Eric Church for Record Year; Post Molone and Morgan Wallen for I Had Some Help; ERNEST and Morgan Wallen for Flower Shops; Luke Combs for She Got the Best of Me; Kenny Chesney for You and Tequila (Karaoke Favorite); Jason Aldean for Tried to Love Me; Jason Aldean and Miranda Lambert for Drowns the Whiskey; Miranda Lambert for Bluebird; George Straight for Run; Alison Krauss for When You Say Nothing at All; Gerry Rafferty for Right Down the Line; Riley Green for Bettin Man and Runnin' With an Angel; Larry Fleet for Where I Find God; Shanandoah for Two Dozen Roses; Travis Tritt for Anymore; Cody Johnson for Stronger and On My Way to You; Matt Stell for

Everywhere But On; Jelly Roll and Lainey Wilson for Save Me; Lainey Wilson for Heart Like a Truck; Muscadine Bloodline for Turn Back Time; Jon Pardi for Ain't Always the Cowboy; Whitney Houston for I Will Always Love You… this is just to name a few.

To Anna Richardson and others at the Green Beret Foundation. Thank you for the service you provide for these Warriors and their families.

NASHVILLE—I love you more than you know. Thank you, Kid Rock and John Rich, for your support for Veterans, for hosting fundraising events for our heroes, and for your unwavering Patriotism displayed on Broadway.

About the Author

Dr. Holmes has more than twenty-five years of experience securing resources and implementing effective programs in diverse settings. She continues to inspire systematic change for practitioners, researchers, and businesses around the world. She is a versatile professional with proven experience in large-scale programs and projects around the world. She has presented on numerous topics at several national and international conferences. Her past work focused on global cultures and social movements throughout the world. She has since directed her focus to the Veteran Affairs program that is broken in America.

Contents

FOREWORD

In 2020, I was reacquainted with a dear childhood friend. This book is not about our many accolades and accomplishments but more about love. The love one has for family, military, and country. Our story has been characterized by many as "The Notebook." Erick and I met when we were eight years old. Like an old country song, "Eight years old, couple cane poles." This was Erick and me.

I would ride on the handlebars of his bike, challenge him to climb the highest limbs in the neighborhood trees, and reciprocate challenges just trying to get the other's attention. He often tells others that he remembers seeing me for the first time and explains how I looked like a pinwheel spinning down the street, cartwheeling it all the way home to my mother's call home for dinner.

We were two little children who had no idea

that our journeys would again cross with a major crisis at hand. I had no idea that his commitment to this country, his sacrifices, and the agreement he made with his country, would not be honored.

Prior to our reunion in 2020, Erick and I crossed paths in 2010 and spent about two hours catching up. We shared our many life stories and adventures, as childhood friends do, and we simply just laughed about life. At this time, I had no idea that he suffered from so much war trauma that had not been addressed.

In 2011, Erick was diagnosed as having PTSD from combat. He served five tours as a triple tab (Airborne, Ranger, Special Forces) in both Iraq and Afghanistan, and was nominated for a Bronze Star. His valor was immeasurable. The service and dedication that he gave to our country was a one-way road.

The services needed for Erick after leaving the military were not available. I was dumbfounded by the lack of services provided by our government. I asked, how is it that a soldier takes an oath to defend, protect, and to serve yet when his service is over, the contract ends. I mean, it fully ends.

An agreement that was once in place is now gone. An agreement that provides a pension but no rule book for life as a civilian. There were no conversations regarding the loss of life, casualties, or debriefs to discuss the chaos or trauma that he experienced in a combat war zone. Instead, my husband compartmentalized all aspects of war. However, he didn't realize he was fighting a new war.

This book was written with love. I wrote this book to help caregivers and family members of combat services members to make them realize they are NOT ALONE.

This book is intended to help others better understand the ongoing crisis on the home front for combat veterans and their families. We must ask, why our loved ones suffer so much when they return home from serving our country. We must understand their military careers from start to finish. We must explore the resources that have failed them at every turn.

Trauma is NOT our fault... but it IS our responsibility to address it.

CHAPTER 1

THE DNA OF A WARRIOR

What is a warrior? A warrior is someone who has engaged in or experienced warfare. These warriors are known for their bravery and skill in combat. We are most familiar with notable warriors, such as:

- Samurai
- Knights
- Spartans
- Vikings
- Ninjas
- Roman Legionnaires
- Zula Warriors

What about Americans born with a legacy of service? This term, not often used, refers to families that have multiple generations of service members. Erick, known as Frederick Earl Holmes, Jr, was born to be a warrior and proved to be just that.

What is in a name?

Erick was named after his great uncles Francis (Freddy) and Earl Duffy. Freddy was a Marine and Earl was in the Army. Both were honored for their bravery during WWII.

Freddy was a Marine who participated in the Battle of Iwo Jima , one of the most pivotal battles in the Pacific Theatre of war during WWII. Freddy fought for the first nine bloody days of the battle before being shot and injured. Due to Freddy's bravery and courage under fire, he and twenty-six other military personnel were honored for their bravery. General Chester Nimitz said,

"Uncommon valor was a common virtue of the men fighting on Iwo Jima." Freddy lived to be ninety-seven years old.

Meanwhile, his brother, Earl Gavin Duffy, a Ranger in the European Theatre of Conflict, played a significant role in the events related to the D-Day landings. The Germans had emplaced a battery of 155(mm) Howitzer guns atop a key piece of terrain overlooking both Utah and Omaha Beach, known as Pointe du Hoc. The notable feature of Pointe du Hoc were the 100 feet above cliffs that had to be scaled immediately upon making the beach landing in order for the guns to be destroyed.

The mission to destroy these enemy positions fell to the Rangers of the 2nd and 5th Ranger Battalion (Provisional Ranger Group), led by Lieutenant Colonel James E. Rudder. Waiting for low tide, this group of men ascended the cliffs with ropes and ladders. Lieutenant General Omar N. Bradley assigned this challenge to Rudder and his Rangers. Bradley stated, "No soldier in my command has ever been wished a more difficult task than that which befell Rudder." This mission contributed significantly to the success of both Utah and Omaha Beach.

Additional ancestry records show that Erick's

lineage of warriors goes back two hundred and fifty years. With his eighth great-grandfather crossing the Delaware River with General Washington on Christmas Eve of 1776. He fought and died in the ensuing battle against the Hessians after having fought in 4 major campaigns in that year. Two of his other great uncles fought at San Juan Hill, along with Theodore Roosevelt, who were a part of the volunteer cavalry unit known as "The Rough Riders."

Erick's maternal grandfather and paternal step-grandfather served in the Air Force during WWII, and three of his uncles, Jimmy (Army), Paul (Navy), and David (Army), all served in the United States Military.

As a child, Erick was fascinated with arranging toy Army soldiers in detail involved battle scenes. He would spend hours maneuvering soldiers in tactical combat action. I remember, as a little girl, him leading the children of the neighborhood in war games. He had a burning desire for military service but did not understand the depth of his connection to his warrior roots and DNA.

Erick attended Florida State University where he studied Geology and was a member of the Army ROTC. Upon Graduation, he was commissioned as a 2nd Lieutenant (2LT) regular

Army Infantry Officer and attended the Infantry Officer Basic Course (IOBC), Airborne School, and Ranger School while at Fort Benning. After his term, he took some time off from the military but wanted more. Since the Military was downsizing, he looked at his options and decided he wanted to become a Triple Tab Green Beret, Airborne, Ranger, Special Forces, known as the Tower of Power.

He went to a Special Forces Assessment and Selection (SFAS), which is an intensely grueling twenty-four-day selection process weeding out over 70% of those who start the course. Those selected, have simply been picked to attend a more grueling one year and a half long process of training, known as the Special Forces Qualification Course (SFQC) to become a U.S Army Green Beret. At this time, he had no idea his family's history, he just knew he was a warrior and wanted more.

Erick was successful in completing the Q course and joined the 20th Special Forces Group (Airborne) (20th SFG) as an Army National Guardsman. He later enlisted and joined the 5th Special Forces Group out of Fort Campbell, KY, where his group was the first into Afghanistan after 9/11. 5th Special Forces Group is known best and portrayed in the 2018 movie "12 Strong."

Erick completed five tours as a Green Beret and was nominated for a Bronze Star (Appendix A) for his heroism. He returned to the Middle East conflict as a contractor. During his service to our country, he sustained both physical and psychological damage. His physical injuries included a severe back injury resulting in many surgeries. He was diagnosed with PTSD due to his exposure to the various combat situations he endured. He also suffered a heart attack and stroke while at war that he was unaware of until years later.

His memories of the war, the guilt of survival and his emotional scars have affected his mental health, quality of life, and relationships, which have been severely hampered due to his repeated exposure to war. And although he was made tough, which is clearly a marker of his DNA, a man can only endure so much trauma, and the effects of the trauma manifest in bouts of violence, extremely risky behaviors, drug use, and deterioration of normalcy for him and his family.

This book is not about pointing out things that Erick has done. He is a Christian man and believes in God. He has often recalled to me his existential inner dilemma, debating whether the sum total of him was good or evil due to so much violence that he visited upon other human beings and the taking of lives.

Understanding how these men are impacted and defining the triggers, emotions, and risky behaviors are only a few steps in recovering. Those who have returned aren't the same and their families are made keenly aware of this by the erratic behaviors of their loved ones upon returning from war.

A sentiment that has been expressed to me in many conversations with other military families is that they were more aware of the severity of the issues than the veterans themselves. Most veterans are either unable to recognize their dysfunction through the fog of war or are unwilling to admit it to themselves or others. Due to social stigmas, they remain in complete denial of any PTSD for years. I saw this with my own husband.

Trauma is NOT our fault... but it IS our responsibility to address it.

CHAPTER 2

MILITARY SERVICE: THE WORLD VS. THE UNITED STATES

Military Service: The World vs. The United States

It is important to understand the sacrifices made by American Citizens and their "voluntary" military service. According to worldpopulationrivew.com, the United States has the "highest defense spending budget of any country, despite the fact that fewer than 1% of its citizens serve."

<u>Countries with Mandatory Military Service 2024 (worldpopulationreview.com)</u>

Most nations have some form of military but vary in terms of how the ranks are filled. Per this global map, there are seven types of recruitment:

- Voluntary
- Mandatory
- Conscription Draft
- Selective Compulsory Service
- De Jure Compulsory Service
- Combination

Israel, along with other nations, requires two years of military service from both males and females, and after their service requirement is complete, they remain on reserves in the event a conflict occurs.

The United States is considered a "De Jure Compulsory Service." When abled-bodied males reach the age of eighteen, they are required to register with the Selective Service in the event a draft is necessary. However, we view the United States as more of a voluntary enlistment based on the fact that citizens choose the military as their employer. This sacrifice is considered the most responsible.

When a United States citizen makes the decision to join the military, it will require a contract, strength, courage, and motivation. Once their decision is made, the news is shared with family and friends. The recruit begins to prepare mentally and physically for this journey. They have committed to a job that will impact their life forever.

There is nothing like shipping a loved one off to boot camp, receiving that first letter or first call, and celebrating their success as they graduate from boot camp. We currently have two sons who are on active duty in the Army and the Marine Corps and have been able to experience this moment with our children. As family members, we wish them a great career in the military and pray for their safety. We find joy in our hearts to see our loved ones in uniform and the pride they exhibit as Soldiers, Marines, Airman, Sailors, and Coast Guardsmen.

While they serve, we honor their services by showing our support to their branch of service. We buy stickers, t-shirts, bumper stickers, and such. The patriotism involved is overwhelming and very emotional for all parties involved. We celebrate our service members and their commitment to the military because it is an honor to be a part of a family that serves this country.

We understand what our service members had to endure to make it to this point and support their decision to choose this career. However, we do not understand the emotions they experience by choosing this career and we don't understand the impact this type of career will have after they are discharged from service. Particularly, those that are deployed to a combat zone.

What Does the Career as a Soldier Look Like?

As a Soldier, every moment of the day is spent preparing for war.

Per the Soldiers Creed: mission first, never

accept defeat, never quit, stay disciplined physically and mentally, train and drill, maintain arms, equipment, and self, be an expert and professional, be ready to deploy, engage, and destroy any enemy of the United States, and serve as a guardian of freedom.

I am an American Soldier.

I am a warrior and a member of a team.

I serve the people of the United States, and live the Army Values.

I will always place the mission first.

I will never accept defeat.

I will never quit.

I will never leave a fallen comrade.

I am disciplined, physically and mentally tough, trained and proficient in my warrior tasks and drills.

I always maintain my arms, my equipment and myself.

I am an expert and I am a professional.

I stand ready to deploy, engage, and destroy, the enemies of the United States of America in close combat.

I am a guardian of freedom and the American way of life.

In most cases, the training involved, the anticipation of deployments, and the lasting effects that exposures to uncommon stimulants have on the brain, are difficult to assess.

No matter what branch of the military, all service members are exposed to war-like scenarios including, live firing, explosives, tear gas, starvation, terrible living conditions, and the demands on a person's physical and mental capacity, which are ruthless. To date, there are many documented cases of debilitating physical injuries, sometimes resulting in death, incurred by soldiers just getting through training. This attrition is even more amplified in the training of Special Operation Soldiers. However, there is little data relating to the mental injuries these soldiers may encounter through this experience.

Research is lacking in the area of *the impact of military training and brain disorders*. Does brain injury for military personnel begin during boot camp? Advance training?

It has been found that some Veterans have PTSD and other injuries, although they never served in a combat zone. What are the influencers behind this pandemic?

Let's look at the Soldiers Creed again but rearranged sections in order to gain a better understanding:

- *Mission first… be ready to deploy, engage, and destroy any enemy of the United States*
- *Maintain arms, equipment, and self… stay disciplined physically and mentally*
- *Train and drill… be an expert and professional*
- *Never accept defeat… never quit*
- *Serve as a guardian of freedom.*

The Creed is to be followed as a guide, to help guide the Soldier. A Soldier understands and follows the above practices daily.

How does the military prepare a warrior?

Step 1: MEPS

The Military Entrance Processing Station, processes all individuals looking to join the military. A series of screenings are conducted in order to determine if a person qualifies for the military. This includes medical, physical, and moral screening. Not all civilians qualify. A job is selected, a contract is signed, and an oath is taken.

Step 2: Vaccines

We won't mention the detrimental effects that the mandated COVID vaccine has had on individuals, but there are other vaccines that were forced upon our military personnel. Some vaccines are required due to the potential for concerns of bioweapons, with Anthrax being one. During the Clinton Administration, the Anthrax Vaccine Immunization Program (AVIP) was established to immunize military and certain civilian personnel with Bio Thrax due to biological weapon threats. To date, little if any, studies have been conducted to see the impact of such vaccines with expedited or accelerated trials.

Step 3: Basic Training (otherwise known as Boot Camp)

During this time, the recruit will learn essential skills, core values, physical training, first aid, weapons training, combat skills, confidence building, and navigation skills.

Per the US ARMY, this training is divided into different phases, and each phase is designed to prepare the recruit to become a fit Soldier for our government.

Becoming a Triple Tab:

Airborne School is a three-week course that entails parachute landing and falls, practice jumps from thirty-four-foot towers and jump week. This experience requires dedication and the desire to be challenged both mentally and physically.

Army Rangers require specific physical fitness requirements in order to successfully complete the course and obtain the tab. An Army Ranger undergoes rigorous training in order to prepare for high-stakes missions in enemy territory.

Special Forces: Green Beret

Becoming a Green Beret involves a rigorous selection process. Special Forces Assessment and Selection (SFAS) is held four times a year with 300 potential Green Berets attending at one time. There are several phases of the selection which include Selection and Qualification (Q Course). Challenges include toughness, physical endurance, and adaptability but the attrition rate is high. The Q course consists of several phases and includes Language Training, SERE (Survival, Evasion, Resistance, and Escape) Exercise, Advanced Special Operations Techniques (ASOT), and Staged Invasion of the Fictional Country of Pineland (realistic exercise). Graduates meet the incredible challenges of difficult training and emerge as part of this elite force.

Erick was selected and went on to weapons training as the 18B Special Forces Weapons

Sergeant and attended the Special Forces Qualification Course (SFQC).

He also successfully completed pre-scuba portion of the Combat Diver Qualification Course (CDQC)—a grueling training challenging the Special Forces Soldier. This course is considered one of the toughest military schools to endure. It is said that one out of three completes the course.

Donning the Green Beret

A Green Beret is highly adaptable and specializes in operating globally to fulfill their mission of freeing the oppressed. They have a unique approach to operating within complex and politically sensitive environments.

They pride themselves on their motto, "De Oppresso Liber," is a Latin phrase meaning "Free from oppression." Their mission is to liberate oppressed people and to fight for freedom.

The Green Beret builds relationships in populations during unconventional missions. They operate in ungoverned areas, facing various challenges and threats. Their skills extend beyond combat. They must develop a cultural understanding by emphasizing an indigenous approach to local populations. They must build relationships and trust. They work in politically sensitive environments and exercise patience. They aid during natural disasters and action goodwill. They weigh risks carefully and balance mission objectives to reduce potential political fallout. More importantly, they demonstrate a commitment from the United States.

Green Berets are considered the most intelligent and most lethal warriors in the world—both feared and respected.

They often face intense combat situations, witnessing violence, loss, and life-threatening events. Due to their specialized skills, they are the first to enter enemy territory. Although these men are elitists, they are vulnerable to injury and often witness casualties of teammates. Often breaching and clearing rooms in Close Quarters Battle (CQB), they often experience an overwhelming force of blistering small arms fire from hostile forces. Due to their combat readiness, they are usually the first boots on the ground during a conflict. They are the MASTERS of Unconventional Warfare (UW).

09/11/2001, The First to Go

The Green Berets played a crucial role in

Afghanistan. After 9/11, US forces invaded Afghanistan in order to dismantle al-Qaeda and to remove the Taliban Regime. The Green Berets were among the first to deploy.

These men never quit but there are consequences to their commitment. They experience more combat exposure than any other military force. During the Vietnam War, there were limits to a soldier's time in battle. They would rotate on a one-year tour to balance the effectiveness of the troops. However, longer deployments increased after 9/11, which resulted in significant effects on the soldiers, both mentally and physically.

In 2007, the US Army changed its deployment policy from twelve months to fifteen months. This change increased the traumatic experiences of these soldiers and their families.

What Impacts Result from Longer Combat Tours?

Combat-related Stress: The longer they stay, the greater the psychological impact of traumatic experiences, which leads to PTSD and other mental challenges.

Ethics Violations: This can occur due to

prolonged deployments. The soldiers' decision-making ability decreases after prolonged deployment.

Family Strain: Intense stress from separation and uncertainty

Although longer combat tours are necessary, they come with a significant cost.

A **Pew Research Center survey** found:

- One out of every ten veterans alive today was seriously injured while serving in the military.
- Three-quarters of these injuries occurred in combat.
- 2.2 million wounded warriors, the physical and emotional consequences of their wounds have endured long after they left the military.
- Veterans who suffered major service-related injuries are more than twice as likely to have difficulties readjusting to civilian life and almost three times as likely to report suffering from PTSD.
- Injured veterans are more critical of government assistance, with half stating that they haven't received enough help.

- <u>Despite these challenges, most veterans remain proud of their service and would encourage young people to enlist</u>[2].

<u>https://www.pewresearch.org/social-trends/2011/11/08/for-many-injured-veterans-a-lifetime-of-consequences/</u>

My first experience with the VA was in 2023, and what we experienced is beyond shameful to the men and women who have selflessly served this nation. The late Toby Keith's song "American Soldier" defines the sacrifices that these men and women make.

> *"And I will always do my duty*
> *No matter what the price*
> *I've counted up the cost*
> *I know the sacrifice*

> *Oh, and I don't want to die for you*
> *But if dyin's asked of me*
> *I'll bear that cross with honor*
> *'cause freedom don't come free"*

How has this nation failed at serving those who so selfishly served us? They fully fulfilled their duty but we have failed them as a nation. Why is our government failing and other private organizations, such as the Green Beret Foundation and Wounded Warriors Project, who are not federally funded but are funded by donations received from civilians serving our veterans more than the government they served?

These organizations provide services and resources to help put a band-aid on the wounds. The physical injuries are addressed by a service member, but what happens when they are discharged from service and receive benefits from the VA? The VA basis compensation on the service-related injury. They offer resources for the veteran but do not have the capacity to serve the veterans in dire need of mental health care.

Addressing physical injuries is easy to address through traditional medical practices, but what about the invisible injuries to the brain? Traditional medicine does not seem to work for those in need of mental health services. Big Pharma is implemented in the VA system and is another Band-Aid approach to helping the veteran, but it comes with many side-effects. Most drugs being used enhance suicidal thoughts. The rate of Veterans who served from 2001 – 2021 has increased from twenty-two a day to forty-two a day.

We must address how the body handles trauma. We must address how long ago the trauma took place and look at each veteran as an individual. These approaches should never be a "one-size fits-all" approach to treatment because each veteran is generally different. They have different backgrounds and different approaches to life. Remember, these men come from a tough mindset, and many believe they can cope with no assistance needed.

Trauma is NOT our fault… but it IS our responsibility to address it.

CHAPTER 3

THE MANY WOUNDS FROM WAR

The Many Wounds from War:

Military is a very masculine career, regardless of your sex. You are expected to "be tough."

At the end of a tour, you are asked—is there anything that happened while you were deployed that you need to talk about or that bothers you?

Per Erick, The Warrior's answer was always NO! They would compartmentalize the "really bad things," pushing them down deep and out of reach for access or processing. This often results in binge drinking, drug use by some, and engaging in risky behaviors, but they were always ready and anxious to return to war.

A soldier takes an oath to protect and stay physically and mentally strong. While the military focuses on a TEAM mindset and morale, what happens when a team member becomes a casualty is injured physically or mentally. How is the morale kept at an effective functioning pace or operational tempo?

There are many elements that need to be addressed in this chapter and we will start with the loss of identity. Adjustment Disorders are prevalent among these men, and they often experience emotional and behavioral difficulties during this transition—from military to civilian life.

Let's face it: Green Berets have massive egos, and when they are no longer able to fulfill their duty, fight for justice and liberation, and free the oppressed, a crisis now occurs.

When in a combat zone, there is no time to stop and think, when do I get a break or a vacation. These men will not stop until they are stopped by injury or death. The scenes of war are never erased; hence, invisible wounds are deeply embedded, particularly in those who go into combat for long periods of time or with multiple tours.

These wounds are presented through various

forms of mental health issues due to the trauma experienced at war, such as flashbacks and nightmares, hyperarousal, avoidance, violence, and addiction.

Trauma is NOT our fault... but it IS our responsibility to address IT.

Erick was a Green Beret, serving five tours and spending ten years in and out of war zones. In 2007, going after a buddy under fire in Helmand, Afghanistan, he endured what would have been to others, a career-ending injury. He blew the lowest disc out in his back and stayed for a month, causing permanent damage to his leg.

After remaining in combat for that month, he returned to the States for back surgery, conducted a hasty four-month rehabilitation for his back, and went straight back to war for four more years.

It should also be noted that he endured a heart attack and a stroke during this period, that he was not aware of, continuing to function as a combat-effective operator for the entire duration of his tours.

The Psychological Wounds from War:

Warriors witness violence, loss, and other unfathomable abuse to humanity. The emotional toll is heavy and is often triggered by symptoms related to PTSD.

Beyond their physical wounds, the toll of trauma prevents their ability to control their impulses, which they had full capacity to do as a soldier, particularly Green Beret. When this trauma is not addressed, the well-being of the freedom fighter now goes into crisis mode.

One of Erick's greatest challenges was to first familiarize himself with the condition of compromised impulse control brought on by years of wrenching the nervous and endocrine system of the body, which renders the "fight or flight" response. Soldiers experience this phenomenon on a constant basis while in combat.

Secondly, we had to develop strategies and methods to identify and manage the potential pitfalls of this condition for Erick and myself.

PTSD is rendered under a "one-size-fits-all" umbrella classification in the psychiatric field. It has been my personal experience that combat PTSD and to a greater degree, Operators Syndrome, are something completely different. This book goes into greater detail about how these classifications differ from other garden-variety

PTSD diagnoses.

Post-Traumatic Stress Disorder (PTSD)

According to DSM-5, the clinical definition for PTSD is "an anxiety disorder that develops in reaction to physical injury or severe mental or emotional distress." PTSD is an injury that most combat veterans, especially operators, will suffer in silence. They took an oath, yet despite the incredible stamina of military operators, the near misses and human casualties takes a toll on the BEST and most ELITE.

Symptoms of PTSD include reoccurring memories, nightmares of the event, sleeplessness, loss of interest, feelings of numbness, anger, irritability, and constantly on the guard (hypervigilance), and emotional distress.

PTSD is trauma that has not been treated and results in anxiety/stress. Factors that increase the likelihood intensity of the trauma, include losing someone you were close to, being physically close to the traumatic event (repeatedly), feeling out of control, and ultimately experiencing a sense of helplessness following the traumatic event.

People with post-war PTSD avoid places that remind them of what happened. Seemingly innocuous things, such as traffic jams and trash piles on the side of the road are triggers, just to name a few.

There are unique stressors associated with military life and after one's service has ended. Most have issues with substance abuse (drugs and alcohol), consider harming themselves or others, and isolate themselves from others. Although the VA offers help for those in a Crisis, the number of Veterans has climbed from twenty-two a day to forty-two a day.

Depression is enhanced by the separation of loved ones and exposure to difficult situations. While anxiety comes in different forms (panic disorders, social anxiety disorder, etc.), it too will present itself in a variety of symptoms for both mental (excessive worry and fear) and physical (rapid heartbeat and sweating).

Substance abuse among combat veterans is a major issue. These men turn to alcohol and drugs to cope; however, substance abuse exacerbates their mental health and reckless behavior.

These operators often experience Traumatic Brain Injury (TBI) resulting from combat. This injury leads to cognitive, emotional, and behavioral changes.

Insomnia and sleep disorders are common due to frequent deployments, irregular schedules, and combat stress. Grief and loss are never addressed, and family and intimate relationships are strained.

Understanding the Chaos:

Preparing for war is one thing but to actually participate in war, is another. Combat PTSD is presented through various forms of mental health issues due to the trauma being untreated. When our emotions are high, we are in survival mode.

For those who engaged in combat, returning to a seemingly unfamiliar society that was once home, is a common sentiment expressed by these veterans.

To gain a better understanding of how this appears to the veteran, we must ask them… how does returning home look? Smell? Taste?

> *Erick's response to me of how it felt to return home was: one of thanks and admiration on one hand from a portion of the population. On the other hand, a surprisingly large percentage of the population were cynical and passively aggressively hostile towards combat*

Things that used to seem familiar to our loved ones are now foreign.

A soldier's homecoming was once a major hallmark found in every town in America, but this support has since disappeared. From protests at university campuses where VA programs are housed (Emory and Vanderbilt), the burning of our flag in the streets, visions of terrorism on our turf, and the scenes from Israel's invasion, all spark flashbacks and reignite their trauma.

The welcome parties for our veterans have disappeared. The VA is overwhelmed and unequipped, *Civilian America* is broken, and our own government, which has sworn to protect our freedoms that these men and women have fought so hard for, aren't prepared to help and rehabilitate those who so selflessly gave so much.

So how is it that our military is trained to go into a firefight to help others but when the firefight is on the home front, the help is a mere band-aid?

How do we bring all of our service men and women home? Before the war, they were outstanding, well-adjusted people with normal lives. Iraq and Afghanistan warzones are what impacted our service men and women. As a soldier, you look to your left and right, you watch out for your team members. What happens when a team member is now a casualty? In the middle of your mission (job), a team member dies, and you are expected to continue on and fight.

Operators and their Approach to Mental Health Care:

According to a 2020 survey conducted by Wounded Warriors Project (WWP), it was found that nearly 60% of military service members suffer from mental health problems but will not seek help. There are many reasons for this number.

One, they are in denial. The social stigma associated with mental illness is a common barrier for civilians but significantly higher among active military and our veterans. They see this as a sign of weakness and that they can tough it out without assistance.

The most disturbing is the lack of access to mental health care. The system in place is overwhelmed. In addition, WWP found that nearly one in five warriors reported difficulty in accessing professional mental health care and two in three warriors felt embarrassed or ashamed to seek care.

https://www.woundedwarriorproject.org/media/z ojlzv53/2020-annual-warrior-survey.pdfWe have an obligation to combat the stigma that these veterans are avoiding and ensure that services are available for those who were in combat zones.

We must help the individual understand that seeking help is a sign of strength and not weakness.

How can family members best support a warrior's mental health journey when resources are limited?

Family members play a major role in the healing process and well-being of their loved one who is struggling with mental health issues related to war. There are different areas that must be considered. We must first understand who they were before the war and how the war impacted them mentally.

How was this warrior before the war in terms of how they handled stress, addiction, relationship factors, family closeness, etc.? Then, we must educate ourselves in regard to understanding the symptoms, triggers, and coping strategies.

We must listen and encourage the warrior to express their feelings without judgement and ask open-ended questions. The few times that Erick conversed with a counselor and decided to open-up about his time in war, the responses triggered his anger.

I remember listening to him tell a story about the day Sergeant Major Stacks died in an ambush. Erick was on the 50 caliber and was pulled off to work another part of the mission. He had arms he had to follow and account for, as he was the 18B (weapons sergeant). Following the instructions of his commander, he jumped down and directed another support serviceman to take his place. He shook hands with Stacks, both agreeing to see each other in about 30 minutes, but that did not happen. Shortly after the convoy pulled away, they were ambushed and all perished.

The counselor responded in a snarky manner, "That must have been triggering. Now, let's move on." He lost it. She had reduced the pain and loss of losing buddies in combat to an inconvenient sidenote to be glazed over.

That upset him greatly and I don't blame him. Upon my own investigation, I found the VA uses inexperienced and unqualified counselors. They had not been in the military, let alone, been in a war zone to be equipped to deal with the uniqueness of these veterans' issues.

Many questions arise here but I must ask the same questions: Why are we putting a Green Beret, who went to war five tours, in front of a twenty-eight year-old counselor to "try" and address his PTSD from war? This is the same response I have heard from many other operators going to counseling for the same.

Common response: ***They have never done what I've done; how can they help me?***

The end result is never a good one. They refuse to return to counseling and usually, go back to what they were doing (risky behavior and addiction issues). The cycle starts over for the family. Back to square one and waiting for the next call for a bailout from their actions (Battery, Domestic Violence, DUI, gambling, etc.).

Discussions of mental health have always been taboo. No one wants to discuss their family battles let alone identify as having their own. I spent years trying to help my mother cope with depression and addiction. The result was she ended her life in 2010. I had to then do my own soul searching and figure out how to prevent this from happening again to a loved one.

First, we must normalize discussions related to mental health issues. We must have open conversations about the topic so that it DOES become the norm. Let's first look at our own behaviors, relationship approaches, addictions, and overall mindset of life. Then, once we understand our own struggles, we can then start to understand others. We must be patient and non-judgmental as we want the same reciprocated.

Warriors will present a series of common behavior issues, such as mood swings, irritability and will withdraw from society. There are many people who did not go to war that exhibit the same behaviors. As mentioned earlier, we must also look at the individual, the family dynamics, and the behaviors of the warrior before war.

We cannot blame or criticize and realize that mental health challenges are not character flaws, as we all harbor some. We can encourage professional help, but again, the response is always the same as mentioned above: **How can someone help me who has never experienced war like I did?**

How do we promote self-care among these warriors when they suffer in silence? They want to be left alone and do what they want until they leave this planet. The pain is deep and we, as family members, love them so much and want them to live a better life with us. We want the old them—BACK. Although that person is no longer there, we honestly believe that they deserve to find peace. Our love for them runs so deep and we hurt when we see them hurting.

How do we minimize triggers?

To begin with, we must look at the current events, societal norms, and our government's approach to the well-being of a combat veteran. I do not wish to elaborate on this as we can all understand that the pull-out from Afghanistan, the invasion of Israel, and the protest on United States soil for terrorists have ignited rage that we can't grasp.

These are elements that we cannot control. So, how do we promote self-care for our loved ones when they struggle with current events?

There are a few approaches to take:

- NO NEWS!!!
- NO Social Media
- Proper sleep, exercise, and relaxation.
- Proper nutrition

How do we help?

- Be aware of potential triggers
- Provide space and solitude for the warrior
- Learn crisis intervention skills
- Recognize warning signs
- Involve the whole family
- Avoid contributing to harmful behavior, if they struggle with sobriety, you must be sober yourself
- Set healthy boundaries
- Celebrate progress and resilience
- Seek support as a loved one
- Advocate for policy change

In Chapter 1, I outlined the training that goes into becoming a warrior. In order to address the mental health issues surrounding a combat soldier, we must readdress the military community that the warrior came from.

The military focuses on a certain culture and values. For example, they emphasize teamwork, loyalty, and sacrifice for the greater good. They will prioritize the mission over their own well-being. The warrior is expected to remain strong, resilient, and unemotional or be deemed as weak, hence, promoting stoicism.

If the warrior experiences any form of mental health breakdown, they fear repercussions and shame. After all, image is everything. Especially when you are a Green Beret. The Green Berets are extremely masculine and have a strong perception of an identity related to masculine norms.

Extended military families serve these men well. However, most of them struggle and will not openly discuss their issues unless court-ordered treatment (forced treatment) has occurred. Then, their approach is mission-driven and they only follow the plan to check the boxes. This approach also prevents proper healing.

Some factors, like ethnic and religious factors, impact the healing process for those with mental health issues. Some view mental illness as a spiritual or family matter. It is frowned upon to discuss in public or with others. Some warriors may prefer traditional healing over Western medicine. However, programs that are expanding for combat soldiers in need are implementing meditation, yoga, and other holistic approaches to healing.

Taking these elements associated with these extremely masculine men, we must find a way to encourage healing practices, and it must be customized to approach mental health based on cultural nuances.

Remember, these men are struggling with reintegrating into a society that is not one in which they are familiar. Their career was constantly preparing them for war. Once the war is over and they are discharged and sent home, their identity must evolve. They are no longer the active-duty Green Beret, Ranger, or a soldier. They must transition into the role of the former operator and mentor of generations of warfighters to come. They will find renewed purpose in passing on the knowledge and experience from their military service in the theatre of combat.

Currently, our government does not address mental health during this transition. The VA does not monitor the condition of the veteran as he is transitioning into the civilian world. Instead, they help them transition from being a warrior to a civilian—From Joe (GI Joe) to a John (John Doe).

These men who used to be so recognized in the military family are now in a culture where they must forcefully identify who they are.

So how do we help our warrior recover from trauma?

First, we must avoid enabling negative behavior, particularly substance abuse and other risky behavior. We also must prioritize our own well-being. Supporting someone with PTSD can be emotionally draining and very costly in the legal realm of things.

Again...

Trauma is NOT our fault... but it IS our responsibility to address it.

CHAPTER 4

UNDERSTANDING THE TRAUMA

Understanding the Trauma:

While studying psychology at the University of South Florida, I remember analyzing the impact of trauma when not addressed. In many cases, children who were abused as children develop various disorders due to not addressing the trauma. Whether it is from physical, sexual, or emotional trauma, it impacts the psyche.

The impact of the trauma will depend on the age of the person when the trauma first occurred. When a person struggles to overcome trauma, it will manifest and often lead to addiction, depression, anxiety, identity disorders, and sometimes, suicide.

This was the case with my mother. She suffered

from both physical and sexual abuse as a child because her trauma was never addressed properly. She struggled with addiction issues and eventually took her own life in 2010.

I suffered my own trauma from childhood that did not manifest until I was in my 40s. I refused to use the same system that failed my mother and so many others.

I found an alternative. I started to study under a five-step method, Brain Education, which was systemized by a Korean, named Ilchi Lee. This program taught me the importance of the brain and how we must experience self-worth and learn to discover one's life purpose. I learned how to "peel the onion" back (expose my pain) and address my trauma at a deep level.

This process took me on a journey where I had to learn to forgive those who I did not feel deserved my forgiveness. This program taught me how to look at my feelings and address my emotions through different holistic techniques. With this approach, a person must commit to practicing every day.

I shared many books and techniques with Erick, and some worked. He understood that the only way to heal was to implement these practices and techniques daily.

In order to get a Green Beret to listen to something that seemed like a feminine approach to healing, I referenced this new type of training to his commitment and training as a Special Forces soldier. Meaning, he was required to stay in shape both mentally and physically. However, there were multiple variables that needed to take place for this process to work.

First, we must address all elements that the VA has publicly recognized as disorders found in Veterans.

Approximately **11%** of veterans who visit a medical facility run by the Department of Veterans Affairs (VA) for the first time have a substance use disorder (SUD). According to these findings, binge drinking or consuming a lot of alcohol in a short time is one of the more common issues that veterans face.

Veterans may abuse substances in response to mental health disorders, to cope with readjusting to civilian life, or to manage pain.

Substance use has been linked to trauma, homelessness, mental health disorders, physical health issues, increased risk of suicide, and problems in relationships and at work.

Statistics on substance abuse in veterans show that among those who have SUDs:

- More than 80% (nearly 900,000) abuse alcohol.
- Nearly 27% (about 300,000) abuse illegal drugs.
- About 7% (almost 80,000) abuse both alcohol and illegal drugs.

There are additional statistics that are alarming.

Alcoholism:

Alcohol abuse and binge drinking are common among active-duty military personnel, and this behavior may continue and turn into alcoholism after separating from service.

According to statistics on Veterans and substance abuse, veterans who abuse alcohol are at greater risk of experiencing or committing violence, suffering from negative health consequences.

Per Veteranaddition.org:

- Alcohol is the primary substance for 65% of

veterans entering treatment centers—nearly twice the rate of civilians.

- Male veterans are more than twice as likely to be diagnosed with an alcohol use disorder (AUD) than female veterans.
- In 2018, 25,000 veterans aged 18-25 had an AUD in the past year.
- In 2018, 874,000 veterans aged 26 or older had an AUD in the past year.

Drug Use:

Drug use among veterans can include illicit or prescription drug abuse. Prescription opioids, which may be prescribed to manage service-connected injuries or chronic pain, have the potential to lead to abuse or addiction.

- Marijuana is the most commonly used drug, with 3.5% of veterans reporting use in the last month and 2.3 million veterans (11.1%) reporting use in the last year.[1,2,4]
- Nearly 11% of veterans were admitted to treatment centers for heroin use.[1]
- More than 6% of veterans were admitted to treatment facilities for cocaine use.[1]
- Male veterans are twice as likely to develop an addiction to drugs than female veterans

(due to the intensity of the war experiences of combat arms soldiers in comparison to those of other soft-skill MOS's)

- In 2018, 45,000 veterans were diagnosed with an addiction to heroin.[4]
- In 2018, 41,000 veterans were diagnosed with an addiction to painkillers.[4]
- Veterans are most likely to misuse hydrocodone (Norco, Vicodin).[4]

Rolling Stone published an article, "Pentagon Finally Stops Hiding Military Overdose Epidemic," where it was noted that 15,293 overdoses and 332 deaths over a five-year period forced the top brass to admit there was a problem.

Is this problem with veterans compounded by using various substances while on active duty? If so, is this why addiction continues after their service is completed?

What is happening in our military and why are our veterans suffering from mental health issues while employed by our United States Federal government?

But based on the information mentioned previously, this issue may start while under the supervision of our government and if so, why is it not being addressed?

How do we fix this issue when our government is responsible, fails to help military personnel while in service, and more importantly, fails the veterans when they depart from service?

Per Veteranaddition.org:

Mental Health

Mental illnesses such as depression, anxiety, and PTSD can lead to substance use.

The presence of mental illness and SUDs, also known as co-occurring disorders, is especially common in veterans. According to this site, Efforts to self-medicate symptoms or manage stress make vets more prone to developing SUDs.

These mental health diagnoses can result from any combination of factors: genetic predisposition, the stresses of being deployed, exposure to combat and traumatic events, injuries, and the challenges of reintegrating into civilian society.

- Between 82-93% of veterans who served in Afghanistan and Iraq with an SUD had at least one co-occurring disorder.
- Veterans who have an SUD are three to four times more likely to be diagnosed with

depression.[2]

- Approximately 37-50% of veterans who served in Afghanistan and Iraq were diagnosed with at least one mental illness.
- Nearly 10% of veterans have symptoms of anxiety, while about 11% have symptoms of depression.

Erick and many of his compatriots in special operations and combat arms at large, experienced multiple deployments. It can only be imagined the intensification of symptoms that multiple tours would have on these warriors.

PTSD

Combat PTSD results in having your life threatened while in combat. Symptoms can be long-lasting and affect different areas of the person's life, such as sleep, employment, social relationships, driving, and the ability to participate in some activities.

Veterans with PTSD may start drinking or using drugs to try and relieve symptoms. Per this site, if a person already has an issue with substance abuse, it may worsen when a soldier develops PTSD.

Per Veteranaddition.org:

- Nearly 25% of veterans have PTSD.
- Veterans who have an SUD are three to four times more likely to be diagnosed with PTSD.
- Among veterans with SUDs who served in Afghanistan and Iraq, 63% also had PTSD.
- More than 20% of veterans diagnosed with PTSD have co-occurring disorders.

As outlined above, the commonality problem with combat veterans is self-medicating and suffering in silence is their solution to avoid the emotional pain endured from war and physical injuries from war.

How do we approach this problem when the government is part of the problem?

There are many private organizations designed to help veterans but why? Why does our government not provide the service needed for those who volunteered for their country, but private citizens donate and support those who volunteered to serve and protect?

Many programs aid warriors and suggest many types of activities that are done as a team, which is a common facet of their career. However, if the trauma is not addressed, any of these activities potentially have a triggering mechanism that is not always forthcoming.

There is one more factor that prevents this type of soldier, particularly a special operator, from engaging in these activities for healing. The level of frustration goes into overdrive because there are other underlying conditions that have yet to be discussed in an open forum.

To readdress the term Combat PTSD, further research has been done to understand why special operators are suffering more than any other MOS (Military Occupational Specialty) in the military. As outlined in the Rolling Stone article mentioned previously, these operators are showing larger numbers of addiction and overdoses while on active duty.

Surprisingly, others have also investigated the mental health of special operators and the "whys" behind their mental health status during service and after service.

A new term, first defined in 2020 by Dr. Christpher Frueh, has been floating around but has not been recognized in the field of mental health. In addition, attention has recently been paid to this term and the symptoms associated with being an operator.

According to Military.com:

Operator Syndrome: Managing High Allostatic Load:

Operator Syndrome:

Operator Syndrome is a term that describes the health and well-being challenges of military special operators. It is caused by the prolonged chronic stress and physical demands of their careers. It can affect their physiological, neural, and neuroendocrine systems, as well as their psychological, behavioral, and social functioning.

Operator Syndrome refers to a set of medical and psychological challenges faced by U.S. military special operations forces (SOF) personnel. These elite operators endure intense physical and mental demands, including frequent combat deployments and exposure to high levels of stress. The term encompasses a range of symptoms resulting from chronic stress and the physical demands of a military career. Some of these symptoms include traumatic brain injury effects, endocrine dysfunction, sleep disturbance, substance abuse, depression, and more.

So, what makes this syndrome different from PTSD, addiction, or any other mental illness associated with combat or military service?

There are three key factors associated with Operator Syndrome, and to gain a better understanding of what happens to the body, brain, and psyche, we must understand three factors and how these factors are intertwined: Allostatic load, functional impairments, and how holistic approaches promote healing.

First, addressing the allostatic load factor.

This term refers to the cumulative impact of chronic stress and physical demands on the body. SOF operators are expected to maintain high-intensity physical fitness training, adapt to operational stress, absorb trauma exposure, overcome disrupted sleep, and survive poor nutrition.

When these factors accumulate, they lead to chronic stress, resulting in what's known as allostatic overload. Operator Syndrome can be seen as the natural consequence of an extraordinarily high allostatic load. So, in Erick's case, five tours took a toll on both his body and mind and his sense of mental peace and well-being.

Operators with this syndrome experience a range of interconnected health and functional impairments, including:

- Traumatic brain injury effects
- Endocrine dysfunction
- Sleep disturbance
- Chronic pain (joint/back pain, orthopedic issues, headaches)
- Substance abuse
- Depression and suicidal thoughts
- Anger and hypervigilance
- Challenges transitioning from military to civilian life
- Cognitive impairments
- Vision and vestibular issues
- Existential concerns
- Problems with sexual health and intimacy
- Marital, family, and community dysfunction

(Military.com: ***Operator Syndrome: Managing High Allostatic Load***)

So how does a special operator heal from this type of trauma?

A Holistic approach to healing includes

comprehensive, intensive programs that are needed to address the unique needs of SOF operators suffering from Operator Syndrome. However, they do not exist. Some of the programs will practice meditation, yoga, Tai Chi, nature walks, etc., but they fail to explore the root cause of the emotion that is attached to the trauma.

Again, this condition has yet to be recognized in the mental health world but is being used and recognized among active duty and veterans seeking treatment.

Keep in mind, that Operator Syndrome hasn't been officially recognized, but understanding the impact is necessary to care for these men.

Although their experiences can foster empathy from everyone, open dialogue and trust in mental health or rehabilitative centers are missing. These men DO NOT TRUST anyone. This is a direct reflection of the hypervigilance Erick, and others were required to demonstrate when at war.

So, how do we get the operators to practice a holistic approach to healing when they are the most elite men in the military?

The lifestyle must change. Practicing holistic approaches must be practiced daily.

How do we, as caregivers, move past the issues at hand to start the healing process?

There are many issues that have occurred here. And again, this book is not about pointing out the limitations of the VA as it struggles to provide effective services for Erick and other soldiers like him, but it is about addressing the process of healing. We must acknowledge how these cycles quickly spiral due to the underlying issues of PTSD and the causal behaviors stemming from the PTSD that can be better addressed.

Supporting someone with combat PTSD can be emotionally draining. As caregivers, we must build resilience. We must also seek individual therapy and support from outside sources.

I would often find myself withdrawing from Erick, especially during intimate moments. My emotions would kick in, and I would forget about the many elements affecting our storybook love, potential TBI effect, anger issues and hypervigilance, and my own issues that I was learning to cope with.

We have a connection that is very deep (each other's first love) and I knew, deep down, that the spiritual nature of our love's connection, would persevere through these hard times if we never quit on each other and we didn't. After all, these two simple words, NEVER QUIT, were the ethos that Erick adopted, succeeding in the world's toughest military training and unbelievable ten years in and out of combat war zones. This is the same ethos that I brought to him when describing my love for him and the nature of our commitment to this marriage.

How can a Holistic approach help?

One of the statements that I learned while working with Iilchi Lee's Brain Education program was this, ask yourself—do you want the lion to come out of the woods and attack you or a gnat?

In other words, how big is the problem that we are facing and how do we respond to it?

Trauma will manifest and ignite the endocrine system from fear and anxiety. But after practicing Lee's approach to a healthier brain, I learned to adapt to situations as if shooing a gnat away.

Again, this takes time and much practice to get to the point where you do not have an "over-the-top" response.

But before I explain the Holistic approach in

detail in the next chapter but first, I need to outline what the VA claims to offer for all veterans suffering from combat PTSD and addiction.

There are many resources that are intended to help the partners of Veterans with PTSD and other service-related injuries, but getting help and an expedient response from the VA has been nearly impossible.

Beyond unacceptable!!!

Per the VA website, the following programs are designed to help but let's take a closer look at how this information is presented:

1. **National Center for PTSD, Partners of Veterans with PTSD**: The National Center for PTSD "provides information" specifically for partners of veterans with PTSD. It covers how PTSD affects relationships, mental health, and family dynamics.

   This program provides information and does not address the underlying conditions associated with combat trauma.

2. **VA Caregiver Support Program**:
   o The **VA Caregiver Support program** offers services to support family

members who care for veterans. You can reach out to them at **1-855-260-3274**.

- o They provide resources, information, and assistance for caregivers, including those dealing with secondary trauma related to PTSD.

Again, another program offers resources and information but does not address the underlying condition associated with combat trauma.

3. **Vet Center Combat Call Center:**
   - o The **Combat Call Center** is available 24/7 for combat veterans and their families. It provides a space to discuss military experiences or issues related to readjustment to civilian life. **1-877-WAR-VETS**

I have personally reached out to these resources and found they are a dead-end resource for those in need. As a matter of fact, I called the crisis line on a Friday evening only to be advised that I should call a local number on Monday. I was provided a number, and was advised that they were closed, and would not open until Monday at 8 a.m.

How can this be? I did not need the service but tried it to see what they are claiming to do for Veterans. NOTHING!!!

How and Why?

For the most part, the world knows about our 9/11 but is unaware of the veterans who have been affected by war since 09/11/2001.

Approximately 2.77 million service members were deployed for war operations in Afghanistan and Iraq, with the Army accounting for the majority of the deployed. It's important to recognize the sacrifices and challenges faced by these veterans as they transition back to civilian life.

Of those who have returned home, approximately 30,177 have committed suicide compared to the 7,057 who were killed during a military operation post 9/11. Of those suicides, 22, 261 were of those who served in combat. Again, I must ask this question, what is going on with our military? The numbers of suicides for veterans and active-duty personnel are outpacing those of the general population. WHY? HOW?

As discussed in previous chapters, does military training impact the brain? What is increasing the use of alcohol and drugs among members of our armed forces? What medical and emotional factors are connected to these suicidal ideations?

How is the Department of Defense addressing these numbers and current issues affecting the mindset of our military personnel?

Here is what the VA offers:

The Department of Veterans Affairs (VA) provides various benefits and services to disabled veteran:

1. **Disability Compensation**:
2. **Specially Adapted Housing and Grants**:
3. **Service-Disabled Veterans' Insurance (S-DVI)**:
4. **Veterans' Mortgage Life Insurance (VMLI)**:
5. **Vocational Rehabilitation and Employment (VR&E)**:
6. **Education Assistance**:
7. **Dependents' Educational Assistance (DEA)**:

Remember that the VA aims to support disabled veterans and their families through a range of services and benefits. However, not one mention of any specific resources for veterans who suffer from service-connected mental health conditions, such as combat PTSD or substance abuse is adequate.

Per the VA, **Veterans with service-connected mental health conditions can access various resources through the Department of Veterans Affairs (VA):**

VA Mental Health Services:

- **Access VA mental health services** for conditions such as **post-traumatic stress disorder (PTSD), depression, grief,** and **anxiety**. You can use some services even if you're not enrolled in VA health care.
- **Immediate Support**:
  - **Veterans Crisis Line**: Connect with caring, qualified responders for confidential help. Dial 988, then select 1, start a confidential chat, or text 838255. If you have hearing loss, call TTY: 800-799-4889.
  - **Emergency Options**: Call 911, go to the nearest emergency room, or visit your nearest VA medical center.
- **Access Mental Health Services:**

- o **VA Medical Centers**: Call or walk into any VA medical center anytime, day or night.
- o **Vet Centers**: Visit any Vet Center during clinic hours.
- o **Phone Support**: Call 877-222-8387 (Monday through Friday, 8:00 a.m. to 8:00 p.m. ET). If you have hearing loss, call TTY: 800-877-8339.

We have repeatedly reached out to the VA for referrals to treatment centers and disappointedly had to resort to private health insurance to acquire timely service for Erick.

His PTSD, TBI, and additional issues make programs unsuccessful for warriors like Erick because no one has addressed the impact of Operators Syndrome. Operators are the most elite men in our military, and they refuse to show any sign of weakness. And treatment for PTSD is considered a weakness. We tried various coping techniques to help with managing his triggers, which we saw a modicum of success with, which is in direct contradiction to the assessments given by various treatment centers.

Mindfulness, deep breathing to control his nervous system, grounding techniques such as focusing on his senses (seeing, hearing, smelling, tasting, and feeling), and progressive muscle relaxation techniques (couples' yoga) in order to reduce the physical tension he possesses.

I noticed that when Erick experienced an episode, he would halt or pause taking deep breaths. When we first started, things like airports, sporting events, and very crowded spaces would trigger him. COVID restrictions were especially triggering. He cannot fly DELTA to this day, much like the SEAL Team 6 member who took out Bin Laden. In retrospect, given the information the American public has been made aware of with regards to the farce perpetrated by the government. These guys weren't so wrong, were they?

Coping strategies vary from person to person, and veterans who have experienced traumatic events during their service may encounter various triggers that evoke memories or distress related to their experiences.

Triggers include sounds (fireworks, gunshots, and sirens), sights (anything that resembles traumatic events like traffic jams and garbage piles on the side of the road), and more importantly, television shows and social media (coverage related to war evokes distress).

There were two recent events that sent Erick into a spiral, the day that the United States left Afghanistan and the October 7th attack on Israel.

Even when such trauma has been treated, it is important to recognize that other factors may trigger combat PTSD. Certain conversations about memories and emotions, conflict and anger can trigger distress, and unexpected or unwanted touches may induce anxiety.

Since each person's triggers can be unique, especially operators, we must find the right coping strategies to manage the triggers effectively.

As Dr. Frueh has addressed the term Operators Syndrome, we must go further into additional issues that Green Berets are faced with during combat situations.

Here are some key points related to TBI within the Green Beret community:

1. **Study Results:**
   o In 2019, the Green Beret Foundation collaborated with the Department of Neurosurgery at the Icahn School of Medicine at Mount Sinai to study TBI and Spinal Cord Injury (SCI) risks

among U.S. Army Special Forces (SF).

- o Brain and spine trauma pose a severe and enduring threat to Green Berets, accounting for 60% of all Special Operations casualties.

2. **iCare Protocol:**

- o The iCare protocol, developed over the past decade, aims to alleviate TBI symptoms, persistent post-concussion syndrome (PCS), and Operational Stress Injury (OSI, formerly known as PTSD).

The long-term health goals of a Green Beret is the mind, body, and spirit. Various programs have been designed to help the Green Berets to recover and reach their maximum rehabilitation potential (MRP). Continued research, support, and awareness of TBI and the effects of this injury are needed. TBI affects more than just short-term memory, it impacts their daily life, relationships, and overall well-being.

Green Berets, like other military personnel, should be aware of the specific symptoms of Traumatic Brain Injury (TBI).

The symptoms include:

1. Physical Symptoms (headaches, dizziness, sensitivity to light and noise)
2. Cognitive Symptoms (memory problems, confusion, slowed thinking)
3. Emotional and Behavioral Symptoms (irritability, anxiety, depression, sleep disturbances)
4. Sensory Symptoms (vision changes, hearing problems (tinnitus)
5. Motor Symptoms (weakness or numbness, difficulty speaking)
6. Seizures
7. Personality Changes (behavior, personality, social interactions)

While it's challenging to completely prevent Operator Syndrome, given the nature of special operations work, there are strategies and preventive measures that can help mitigate its impact.

Remaining physically fit and conditioned and having a balanced diet supports recovery. Finding a way to manage stress through mindfulness and relaxation techniques, such as meditation, deep breathing, and Yin Yoga (used for muscle relaxation) are key to reducing stress.

The Department of Defense is not prioritizing

the operator's health due to the high number of high-stress deployments, which leads to burnout. In addition, when the operator is transitioned back into civilian life, the VA is lacking.

There are no regular health assessments that are conducted or ways to track symptoms related to Operators Syndrome. This syndrome is multifaced and needs a comprehensive approach that involves both the operator and the organizations for which he is operating. Currently, this approach is missing.

Traditional medicine and VA care vs Holistic approaches

For the VA's approach to care, they promote the use of BIG PHARMA!

There are specific medications the VA uses to help manage PTSD symptoms. In other words, BIG PHARMA! So how are pharmaceuticals used to treat trauma? It doesn't. It masks the emotions. Erick refuses to take the medications because they make him feel lifeless. Remember, these men were hard-chargers (still are), and they do not want to be "put out to pasture" just yet.

Holistic and natural remedies for **PTSD** may not replace professional treatment, but they can complement other approaches and help manage symptoms. I must advise you to always consult with your healthcare provider before trying any natural methods, but we have tried these methods and they work.

The most common approaches include:

- Self-care
- Mindfulness and relaxation techniques (meditation and yoga)
- Healthy diet (nothing processes and juicing to encourage intake of fruits and vegetables)
- Herbal supplements (teas and essential oils promote relaxation)
- Physical Activity (regular activities improves the mood and reduces anxiety)
- Herbal substitutes in place of pharmaceuticals (medical cannabis)

Studies have shown that medical cannabis helps with PTSD symptoms such as hyperarousal, sleep disturbances, nightmares, anxiety, and depression.

Experimenting with different types of cannabis have found that sativa increases his anxiety while the indica has more of a calming effect. The problem is that the calming effect is not what a Green Beret is looking for. They need an adrenaline rush, but I can say this has been a great resource for calming him when needed.

We have also discussed the use of psilocybin therapy, which involves using the hallucinogenic substance derived from magic mushrooms, shows promise in treating various mental health conditions. Responses to psilocybin vary widely among individuals. Although this type of therapy is being used, ongoing research continues, and it has yet to be legalized in the United States.

The newest approach to treating TBI:

I recently visited a Doctor in Atlanta and during our visit, we discussed Erick and his condition. She mentioned NAD. She advised how this treatment was being used for NFL players who suffered from concussions.

Since concussions can leave players disinhibited (more prone to aggressive behavior), the dysfunction of the amygdala (part of the brain that regulates rage) is said to contribute to this effect.

In addition, chronic traumatic encephalopathy (CTW) is associated with repeated brain injuries (like concussions) and can lead to symptoms like impulsivity, explosivity, and aggression.

I mentioned this to Erick, and he opted to try this method. We have seen a difference in various parts of his behavior.

So, what is NAD?

NAD stands for nicotinamide adenine dinucleotide, which is a molecule that occurs naturally in the human body. It plays a crucial role in various physiological processes.

Why is NAD important for Combat Veterans?

As we age, our NAD levels decrease. Depletion of NAD has been linked to age-related conditions such as cognitive decline, cancer, and sarcopenia (loss of skeletal mass and strength). In summary, NAD is a fascinating molecule with potential benefits for longevity and overall health.

We have found that traditional approaches to these warriors do not work. This chapter was to compare the methods being used to treat combat soldiers. The next chapter will identify ways to use holistic approaches to help the brain and body heal.

Trauma is NOT our fault... but it IS our responsibility to address it.

CHAPTER 5

HOLISTIC APPROACH TO HEALING

For the most part, humans are in a quest for optimal health. So, if such trauma, as described in the previous chapters, manifests and is not treated through conventional approaches, how do we regain a proper balance in our lives without leaning towards a vice?

If trauma is not addressed, it will manifest through means of addiction, depression, or anxiety. To heal the body, we must consider the whole person – the body, the mind, the spirit, and the emotions.

So, what is meant by the "whole person?" I took a class at one of the Brain Centers called "Finding True Self." This class was beyond beneficial to me as I had to address trauma from my past and try to figure out who I really was. You see, life took a toll on me and over time, I was a different Neysa to different people. I was different around my parents than my children, different around my coworkers and friends, and I truly lost who I was.

So how do we ask ourselves to find our true selves?

- We must first learn to quiet the mind and become very still.
- We must realize who we are, and NOT who we want to be.
- We must ask ourselves— what are we passionate about?
- We must assess all relationships and how they are impacting our well-being.
- We must learn to meditate and practice these concepts every day.

One of the most important factors we want to achieve in searching for who we are is making sense of our past. We must be able to address the trauma, which will allow us to figure out why we act the way that we do.

We must be able to differentiate between the different people we have become over time and look deeply into who we want to be ALL THE TIME. During the process, we must focus on the positive elements in our lives and learn to remove any negative tendencies in life, focusing on unwanted thoughts and behaviors.

We must recognize our own powers. When we want to achieve something, like becoming a Green Beret, a Ranger, or a Special Operator, we know the challenges but are willing to take on those challenges in order to achieve this goal. For those that achieve this goal, are considered elite and are willing to continue to improve in their craft.

If you were to ask these men if this was the most difficult task they have ever endured, they would say yes. However, the trauma exposure from combat seems to be the most difficult to overcome, as noted in the other chapters of this book. Veterans are struggling to find their true selves and return home as someone else.

How do we use a holistic approach to address trauma? We must first make sense of our past. This is a difficult task, but it is considered a BRAVE task. When we are willing to explore your past and combat the trauma resulting from our past, we can manifest a precious life.

We must first expand the mind with new knowledge.

"Knowing yourself is the beginning of all wisdom."

- Aristotle

Addressing any vices is the first step to differentiating between the things that are good for you and those that impact your body and mind.

What vices do we find destructive? We must internalize the true harm and address the mindset that these vices are good for us.

Understand the Human Body and the Brain

There are many vices to consider when addressing issues associated with Veterans, but alcohol is the most common and seems to have the greatest impact.

As mentioned earlier, Alcohol use disorder (AUD) is a significant risk factor for suicide among veterans who drink alcohol. This chapter explains the various holistic approaches that can be used to help remove addictive vices, using alcohol as an example, is important for many reasons.

So how does alcohol affect the human body and the brain?

1. **Brain**:
   - Alcohol interferes with the brain's communication pathways, affecting mood, behavior, and cognitive function. Consuming alcohol makes it harder to think and impairs coordination.

2. **Heart:**
   - Excessive alcohol consumption can damage the heart over time. Studies have shown that problems include cardiomyopathy (stretching or drooping of the heart muscle), arrhythmias (irregular heartbeat), and high blood pressure.

3. **Liver:**
   - Heavy drinking takes a toll on the liver. Drinking alcohol can lead to fatty liver (steatosis), alcoholic hepatitis, fibrosis, and cirrhosis.

4. **Pancreas:**
   - Alcohol causes the pancreas to produce toxic substances, leading to pancreatitis, and impairing enzymes and hormone production for digestion.

5. **Cancer:**
   - Alcohol consumption is associated with several types of cancer such as head and

neck cancer, esophageal cancer, liver cancer, and breast cancer.

We are advised to drink in moderation; however, the overall health risks affect mental and behavior disorders and alcohol dependency (a vice). If we have a quest for optimal health, how do we remove a vice like alcohol from our lives?

Meditation

Discovering mindfulness is difficult but over time and practice, a person can train the brain to focus on thoughts and activities. We must bring awareness and mental clarity to achieve an emotional calm and stable state.

We ultimately are searching for means to find peace and clarity in our lives, removing all chaos and vices. Current research shows the effects of mediation and how it impacts a person's health. There are many different approaches to meditation, and each person will differ in how they approach using meditation as a part of the healing process.

Mediation significantly reduced stress, anxiety, depression, and pain. This approach to healing may sound farfetched and many people ask: how can thinking, heal the body? As this book has outlined, other methods do not work and implore unhealthy habits (vices).

"Big pharma" is not the solution to healing body. Most veterans lived a great life while in the military before becoming injured. After their injury, the recommendation by the VA is to mask all underlying issues, such as PTSD or Operators Syndrome, by the use of pharmaceuticals unhealthy drugs. This statement is beyond my option. Have you ever paid attention to commercials advertising pharmaceuticals for various ailments? The list of side-effects is longer than a dissertation (i.e., stroke, heart attack, lymphoma, suicidal thoughts, etc.).

So why is mediation so important in the healing process for veterans? There are many options, approaches, postures, and flexibility. Most believe that mediation can only be done while sitting in a lotus position on the floor, but this is not feasible for non-mobile injured or have other issues preventing this position.

Meditation can be done while walking or lying down. The frequency will also vary depending on how in-depth the session is. Depending on the technique used, twenty minutes a day of meditation is extremely beneficial for anyone, but eight minutes a day will also work. The key is to practice daily. It is very important to stay focused and retrain the brain. After all, we are using this approach to be mindful of our thoughts which in turn will change our behavior.

Resources for learning how to meditate can be found on YouTube, applications on your phone, or a traditional center offering meditation, yoga, and Tia-Chi.

Yoga is another holistic approach to healing the body. There are two different types of yoga—Yin and Yang. Yang is more external, dynamic, warming, and upward (strength training). Yin is more internal, passive, cooling, and downward (on the floor). Yin is the most commonly used for those with PTSD and Operators Syndrome because the practice is used to calm the body through breathing and holding poses that release stress/tension in the body.

Erick and I have used couples yoga as a calming mechanism, and he has found improvement in sleep and relaxation.

The final holistic approach to healing that I recommend is the use of essential oils and massage therapy. We have found many essential oils that work. The choices can be that of many but the ones we have used that seem the most beneficial are lavender, jasmine, and geranium. Adding vanilla to each has been found to enhance a more relaxed mixture, especially when using an oil diffuser.

Lavender is used to relax and calm and is wonderful when used at night. This oil is used to promote a peaceful environment. Jasmine is known for reducing stress and anxiety, increasing energy levels, and promoting better sleep. Finally, geranium is used to reduce feelings of stress, anxiety, sadness, fatigue, and tension. All three are beneficial to be used anytime to help reduce anxiety, depressions, and bring calm to a place where someone is trying to heal their body, mind, and soul.

I can speak of these methods and can attest to the benefits. I have trained under the best, Ilchi Lee, to name a few. His method of healing has been the only method that helped me to work through my personal trauma. I took this knowledge and have shared it with many, including Erick.

The purpose of this book was to address the difficulties veterans face in returning from war and the struggles they face reacclimating back into the civilian community. Not only do they suffer from the physical injuries of war, but the psychological impact has resulted in many ending their own lives, struggling with addiction, and revolving through a legal system that fails to address their needs.

This book has outlined the many resources that the VA is supposed to offer but they have been unsuccessful at so many levels. The alternatives are promising but are not an option for the VA to use. Instead, they resort to methods of "so-called" care, that have left our veterans behind.

The Latin phrase "nemo resideo" or "leave no one behind" has been forgotten. This journey has been especially difficult for those who were at the operator's level, struggling with PTSD, addiction, and other elements impacting them from living a more peaceful life.

These are the toughest men, and we as a nation can and should do better. I will continue to advocate for changes in our system aimed at supporting our veterans.

If we, as a nation, commit to pursuing this goal

of NO VETERAN being LEFT BEHIND with the same love in our heart as I had as a little girl looking at that little boy, my first love, growing up in that central Florida neighborhood, we CANNOT FAIL!!!

We owe them honor, respect, and gratitude.

Appendix A

NARRATIVE RECOMMENDTION FOR AWARD OF THE BRONZE STAR TO STAFF SERGEANT FREDERICK E. HOLMES

For exceptionally meritorious service while assigned as the Special Forces Senior Weapons Sergeant on Operational Detachment Alpha 553 (ODA 553) from 18 April 2004 to 20 July 2004. Staff Sergeant Holmes' courage, initiative, and hard work proved invaluable to the success of the ODA during Operation IRAQI FREEDOM II. On 30 April, 2004 ODA 553 received time sensitive information on the location of the Mahdi Militia Area Commander for Al Hillah, a key insurgent leader responsible for destabilizing one of the largest provinces in Iraq. Because the insurgent leader would be departing the area shortly, the ODA had to conduct compressed mission planning. SSG Holmes was instrumental in the design and implementation of the plan. During execution of the raid, he was a member of the first assault team to approach the objective. The assaulters were in two vehicles, and before the vehicles came to a halt they were on the ground and moving towards the entrance of the target building. Once inside the main entrance it became apparent that there were numerous potentially hostile personnel in the courtyard. SSG Holmes had the initiative and tactical savvy to understand that these people had to be controlled quickly to prevent them from becoming a threat to the assaulters. SSG Holmes took control of a member of the second assault team and then quickly and efficiently subdued ten personnel. He collected the detainees in one location using the appropriate level of force, screened them to ensure that they were not hostile, and maintained security over them allowing the rest of the assault team to move through the remainder of the target knowing the personnel behind them were secure. SSG Holmes had the discipline and maturity to know that he had to.. hold his position until the team finished their work on the target. SSG Holmes: held this location until the Team Sergeant could evacuate the detainees, get the assault teams back into the vehicles, and account for all team members. Only then did he pull back to the trucks and link-up with the detachment as they pulled off the objective. SSG Holmes' quick thinking, discipline, and leadership enabled the ODA to accomplish its mission and prevented his teammates from becoming casualties inside a target building where gunfire was exchanged at close range, multiple times. SSG Holmes planned and coordinated a multi-national raid on the village of Albu Alwan on 13 May 2004. The village of Albu Alwan had been a constant safe haven for insurgent fighters and command and control elements. SSG Holmes realized this and organized a strike force consisting of air and ground assets from three different nations. Once SSG Holmes' had conducted all the necessary coordination and rehearsals for the assault force, he ensured that the support by fire elements, consisting of two detachment vehicles and two OH- 58D's, were well rehearsed and synchronized. During a continuous Intelligence Preparation of the Battlefield (IPB) process, SSG Holmes realized that the enemy situation and terrain dictated that a robust quick reaction force (QRF) would be needed. He created this QRF out of Special Forces soldiers from two different nations. The overall plan called for a large number of assaulters and support positions to strike six different targets simultaneously. During the execution of the raid, SSG Holmes supported the main Iraqi assault force by providing security and information from his position as well as information from the aircraft overhead. SSG Holmes' hard work, dedication, and planning ability enabled a multi-national force to work through language barriers and other differences to attack the enemy and capture twenty insurgents, with no friendly casualties. SSG Holmes' joined the ODA in the middle of prolonged combat operations, immediately became part of the team, and showed that he had the motivation and leadership to be an asset to the Detachment. Despite the lack of training in the area of Advanced Special Operations (ASO), SSG Holmes eagerly accepted the challenge and started working as a member of a two-man ASO team. During this time, SSG Holmes operated in civilian clothes using indigenous vehicles to gather information on enemy forces. SSG Holmes produced information resulting in successful attacks on two enemy positions where over twenty enemy personnel were captured. SSG Holmes was then able to generate additional intelligence from the raid to include the identities and locations of personnel that attacked United States Special Forces (USSF). In another instance, SSG Holmes planned, organized, and led a six-man reconnaissance patrol on several missions into non-permissive terrain that was almost entirely controlled by insurgents. During these missions SSG Holmes identified vantage points from where the enemy could be attacked using stand off weapon systems. Once these positions were located, SSG Holmes developed a plan for a small group to attack a numerically superior force using hit and run tactics. SSG Holmes' unconventional plan called for moving into the target area under the cover of darkness, attacking the enemy with stand off weapons, and then quickly departing the area before the enemy could react or pinpoint the friendly locations. These raids struck terror into hearts of the enemy forces in the area. SSG Holmes' courage, bravery under fire, and expertise in small unit tactics epitomize the US Army Special Forces. His actions reflect distinct credit upon himself, the Combined Joint Special Operations Task Force-Arabian Peninsula, the 5th Special Forces Group (Airborne), and the United States Army.